The Fresher's Handbook:
How to succeed at university and live the student life in style

Dr Clifton Reed

Copyright © 2017 Clifton Reed

All rights reserved.

ISBN: 978-1542679053

DEDICATION

To those who do not settle for what they have been given and to those who strive to seek and find and not to yield

CONTENTS

Foreword

1	Work	6
2	Exam revision techniques - work smart not hard!	19
3	Making the productive use of your free time	23
4	Finances	31
5	Employability	34
6	Summary and where to go next	40

Foreword

Hello and congratulations on making a positive step towards improving your future! If you are reading this you are probably on the way to what everyone around you is calling 'your greatest adventure', otherwise known as university. There are many study guides on the market to help you get a first or achieve good grades, but I felt that they didn't go far enough. The main aim of this book is to develop you as a person by improving your productivity, efficacy and overall happiness through a number of tried and tested methods.

I am writing this book because I strongly believe that it is not your intelligence that determines your success but how you conduct yourself and the choices you make. I have known many people much smarter than myself who have achieved much less even with significantly greater advantages.

This concept first became apparent to me when I was at the British Army's Officer Selection Board. During the selection process we did numerical and abstract reasoning aptitude tests. I spoke to a physicist from a top 5 UK university and realised that I had got higher marks than him. How could this be possible? I asked myself. When, at the time, I was studying at a very average former polytechnic university.

It turns out the difference was this: Confidence, organisation and persistence. This book has been written to guide you to develop these skills and achieve your potential. In the last few years I have spent significant time developing my confidence and organisational skills which working on persistence and endurance. I currently hold a PhD in Aerodynamics and work in my dream job as a researcher at a top 20 University.

The overall goal of going to university is to get a job when you leave or go on to further study. Many graduates lack the basic key skills to get their desired job so this book includes tips and tricks on how to improve your employability skills.

Your university years will be shortest few years of your life and before you know it, the gaping chasm of the job market will open up before you. Be smart, be prepared and get ahead!

In the pages to follow, I offer hindsight, anecdotes, dos and don'ts of your university years. Laugh, be amused, take the advice (or don't) – at the very least just be informed. Contained within this book are things I wish I would have known earlier and I promise, if used as instructed, will increase your overall happiness, productivity and employability.

1 WORK

While at university it will generally be expected by your lecturers that you undertake some work...I know this sucks but deal with it. This section contains a guide on how get the highest grades through improving productivity, organisation and stress-management.

Productivity and the power of habit

The aim of being productive is to achieve the most tasks/workload in the minimum allotted time. To put this in terms of the student mind-set: The sooner you get your coursework finished, the sooner you can go out/binge-watch your favourite series on Netflix. This chapter contains a series of tools that I have used to maintain focus, increase my productivity and ultimately extend my playtime.
While at university you are effectively training for the world of work. There, 9 to 5 will be expected and you will not be congratulated for leaving the second after your eight hours are done. Those people who achieve the most at university work a nine to five day and play outside of that. Developing the discipline to achieve this will set you above your peers and on to a positive path. With discipline, anything is possible.
Consider this scenario: It is Wednesday afternoon, you have no lectures and a few hours of Netflix sounds like heaven in a mug. Sound familiar? How about the three pieces of coursework that are due on Friday? If you immerse yourself in whatever drivel you're watching you can safely ignore the work, claim that your dog ate it and get an extension. Consider again that university is a training ground for your future, and that how you behave not is a prediction of your future behaviour, do you really want to continue along this path?
Being productive does not mean slaving away at your laptop until 2 am every morning, nor does it mean getting up at 5 am to finish last minute assignments. Productivity is achieving tasks methodically in order to maximise output with the greatest efficiency which in turn minimises stress and makes for happier living.
In order to get your work 'out of the way' so that you can play, you will need to become disciplined. Discipline is just the implementation of habits over time. Just like going to the gym, breaking new habits in may be painful but if applied consistently, success will follow, I promise.
Real and lasting change does not happen overnight. If anyone tells you this assume they are lying and trying to sell you something fraudulently. Lasting

change takes time but doesn't need to be painful. In the following pages there will be tips and tricks to slightly improve your work skills, productivity, happiness and social life every single day.

Consider the analogy given by Tony Robbins in 'Awaken the Giant Within'. Imagine you have a ship which is sailing on the ocean on a desired course. If you adjust the course by a few degrees initially this will make little to no difference in where you end up. But as the journey continues you will become farther and farther from your original destination before you adjusted course. In this metaphor the direction change is the development of your new productive habits. Over time these will become solidified and your achievement will be significantly greater than would have otherwise been the case if you had not changed. With this in mind, let's consider some habits that are worth enforcing.

Leave the phone alone

When you work your phone goes off. Brace yourself, this is going to be hard. Being away from your phone for a few minutes is going to be painful at first because you're so popular and everyone just cannot be without instant contact with you. Or perhaps Facebook will shut down if you don't check it every five minutes.

I tell you this now: You will not die because you haven't touched your phone in 20 minutes but I appreciate how difficult this will be for some so let's start easy. A simple first step is to leave your phone in your room when you go down stairs to make tea, coffee or cocktails. Perhaps you could speak to the people in your house rather than texting them when they are standing three feet away from you. Take up this habit, ask them about their day/plans and before you know it you'll have forgotten that Alice has sent you another image of her mom's cat. 99% of the time you can live without the messages you are sent. This initial breaking of the bond between you and your beloved phone may be difficult but persevere, the rewards are worth it.

When sitting down to work, if this is a particularly awful piece of coursework, keep your phone on flight mode/off and place it somewhere in the room behind you out of sight so that you are not tempted to check it. It is always a good idea to reward yourself through positive reinforcement, so work in 30 minute slots and use checking your phone as a reward. Do not get drawn into conversions, just reply, be polite and inform people that you're working and will 'catch them later'. People love to distract others who are working because it makes them feel better about their apathy.

How did the 30 minute work bursts go? After a few days this will become a default work mode and already you should have achieved more. However, there is another time-thief which lurks in the land of coursework/revision...

Close that browser window!
While searching for cultural styles of indigenous Aztecs you may have stumbled across Topshop's latest clothing line and are deciding which shoes will go best with that dress you bought last week. It is amazing how easily the human mind is distracted, so let's remove one more distraction.

Checking email is as bad as checking your phone if not worse. The texts I get are usually rubbish, the emails I get are usually worse. I hate to break it to you but checking email is not productive. It feels like work, it makes you feel/look important but no, you will not got your 1st class degree by looking at the same message you've already read twice. Reduce checking emails to twice a day, this way you will not waste precious time in front of a computer that you could otherwise spend shopping, exercising or with friends.

To music or not to music...
It is loved my some and hated by others. Some swear by it, others swear at it. Music is used by many as a means of concentration [is there something to tell you why?]. To completely concentrate on your work it is best to avoid too many audible distractions although some sounds (neighbours having sex) do also need to be drowned out! As a compromise I recommend some music without lyrics: All the muting capability of normal tunes but without the distracting element of the speech.

An alternative to music is to use a white noise generator. White noise provides sounds that blurs background sounds and is often used to help babies sleep. There are hundreds of white noise generators available on all app stores to these can be added to your phone. Just remember, if you're using your phone for this purpose, keep it on flight mode or 'do not disturb' mode.

Challenge
Turn your phone off for two hours per day for the rest of the week.

Organisation Tools

The people that appear most intelligent and 'switched-on' may not be, this is where the power of organisation is valuable. There are many tools that will aid your productivity but the more tools you have, the more time that you will be distracted from performing the tasks you're trying to make more efficient. Below are a few highly valuable tools that will be useful for most people.

Google calendar

Google calendar (or any electronic calendar for that matter) is a product that is free and syncs to your smart phone or web browser. It was first introduced to me by two married doctors who had different working patters and busy social lives. This allowed them to work out when their shifts clashed and when they could find time to be together.

Google calendar is particularly good because you can generate multiple calendars, overlay them and share with friends/partners/family. You should also have the app on your phone so that when someone says 'let's have a group work meeting next Tuesday at 2 pm' you can reply with 'okay, I'll put that in my calendar' and actually show up on time. Calendar apps usually give you a warning period that you can specify (default 30 mins) which gives you ample time to crawl out of bed and sprint to your 9am lecture.

A word of advice: Put events into your calendar the second you get them. I usually do this mid conversation, ignore the person I've just made arrangements with and tell them exactly what I'm doing. This temporary rudeness can usually be forgiven more than standing a friend up.

Overall, those who organise gain followers and are more respected than those who are not. With solid organisational skills you will become a beacon of calm in the turbulent world of the disorganised.

Evernote

I cannot for the life of me tell you where I heard of Evernote but at the busiest time of my life it kept me on the side of sanity. For those aware of the common 'to do' list issue of lost paper, Evernote will solve all of these issues. It free piece of well-designed software acts as a series of pages (called Notes) which can be arranged into groups called 'Notebooks'.

The overall mechanism of Evernote is more complex but assume that you've got three pieces of coursework on at the same time, Evernote will help keep your work/research separate while remaining paperless. Furthermore, it is syncable to two different devices before payment is required so you can carry your notes around and can even add to them on the train or toilet, I don't judge. Ideas come sporadically.

StayFocused

Stay Focused is a website site blocker which blocks or gives you a certain amount of time throughout the day on chosen websites. Stay Focused is free, need I say more? The settings are flexible and can be set to only operate during work hours (i.e. 9 to 5) however can destroy an evening on iPlayer of accidently left on out of work hours.

Other tools

Frankly, there are an infinite number of tools available to help guide you towards success and organisation. The Google calendar and Evernote will be the main ones, although habit keepers such as Beeminder will become useful once you start developing your personal skills and begin to challenge yourself to achieve more than you thought possible.

Productivity task
Add all of your lectures, labs, tutorials and tutorials to your electronic calendar so that you know when and where you need to be at any given time. Add Stay Focussed to your browser and block websites such as BBC iPlayer during work hours.

Goal setting

If you have followed the steps above you will already be on your way to an organised and successful future, if you haven't, go back and implement them! What you sow is what you reap!
Goals are the most important step you will take towards your success so read the following section carefully and then read it again. My first experience at goal setting was in secondary school, where I'm quite ashamed to say I was a bit of a tear away. My idea of hard work was remaining in an entire lesson without being thrown out. If I had written more than five lines in a lesson it was considered a minor miracle by the teachers. During what was known as PSHE (Personal, Health and Social Education), since called a variety of other things including citizenship, we were told to set goals for our schoolwork. Being the petulant teenager I scoffed at this idea and labelled the exercise a complete waste of my time. I proceeded to make a very audible mockery of the entire process. Looking back I can now see how wrong I was, or did I just have nothing worth aiming for back then?
I can tell you now goals are the thing that will take you up to the next level. If you don't believe me ask very successful people or look up their testimonies on the web, in books or magazines. Pretty much everybody who has become massively successful in life has set goals to achieve and the below is a brief explanation on how to do this effectively.
Before you invest your time writing out goals, find something you really want to achieve. The ferocity that you will chase a goal is proportional to your success in it! Don't waste time with half-hearted whims but try to find something that you really desire.
One of the most important ways to help you internalise your goals is to write them down on paper. The action of writing something down causes your mind to focus more deeply on the content. How many thoughts do

you think in a day compared to how many you write down? Hence writing them out will make them more significant.

When you're ready to begin follow the steps below.

Specific - Pick something you want to achieve. If it is 'to learn French' make this more specific to 'to book a hotel room and order dinner in French'.

Measurable – Make sure you can quantify your success. How will you know you have achieved your goal? In this scenario you have booked a hotel room and ordered dinner in French.

Agreed upon – The people involved in setting this goal i.e. you and your French tutor are both in agreement to the chosen path. Note that having people to keep you on track is an excellent way to achieve.

Realistic – Ensure you aren't overreaching. In this case don't try to learn 100 new words every day otherwise you will likely struggle and you may fail through over-exertion and neglect other aspects of your life.

Time-bound – Set a date for completion of your set goal. It is essential to have a time-limit on your goal because it gives you a point in the future to aim for.

Putting all of the above together you should have something like:
"By the [date in one month] I will be able to book a hotel room and order dinner in French."

Now that you have goals, let's work out how to make them a reality. What steps will you take to make this happen? If you want to learn conversational French, you might listen to one hour of French phrases every day. This is relatively easy to achieve while sitting on the bus or walking to lectures. You might go to a class once per week and spend two hours there. Another step could be to review your progress on a weekly basis and make weekly goals (see the Week Planning and Your Learning Style sections).
Once you have your goals I recommend you put them somewhere that you will pass several times a day. A bedroom door is ideal or if you are too embarrassed by your flatmates seeing it try the inside of a folder that you use daily. Goals should be also reviewed before bed and when first waking up in the morning to help focus the mind on the task at hand.

Expand your mind

University is a time when you will have exposure to such a wide variety of cultures, subjects and people that you may not have had before. Make the most out of this opportunity because it is unlikely that you will get one similar ever again. I do not suggest spending your best years in the library pouring through old dusty books, I am suggesting is that you make what I like to call 'dead time' productive.

What is dead time? Walking to the shops, hoovering or washing up are all examples of dead time. Times when you are usually staring at a boring task or travelling on a train can be transformed into fantastic learning experiences through the power of audio books!

Audio books have undergone a massive revolution in the last decade from the cassettes you put in your car stereo which read stories to kids on the way to Skegness. Thanks to the sites companies such as Audible, thousands of audio books are available.

It is great to learn subjects that aren't in your area of expertise. When you're in conversation with someone you barely know (don't worry we'll cover that too!), random conversation topics are a great way to continue the conversation and keep it interesting.

If you're not already completely sold, consider this: Would you rather listen to the same song you've already heard twenty times before and will hear another 100 times before you die, or, learn something new with the minimum of effort? More brilliantly still is that if what you're listening to is embarrassing, no one will ever know (unless you choose to tell them).

De-stress: Relaxation and mindfulness for learning and happiness

When you have multiple assignments that are due in the same week it is easy to become overwhelmed. How will I do them in time? Which one to start first? How will I fit it in? This succession of questions is normal and you shouldn't give yourself a hard time for feeling overwhelmed or stressed it is perfectly normal.

When you graduate, there will be times when you become stressed. Your boss will assign you multiple projects and expect them to be completed. The last thing you want in a new work environment is to be perceived as the person who gets stressed and cannot cope as this will not instil confidence from employers and colleagues.

This section contains a few tips on becoming more relaxed, 'present' and able to deal with multiple stimuli such as deadlines in a calm and ordered fashion.

Mindfulness

Originally something that was only practiced by Buddhists and spiritual people, mindfulness is quickly becoming the performance-enhancing tool of the super-successful. Mindfulness can be briefly described as having a 'present state awareness', which essentially means 'not being in your head'.

Every day, all day, thoughts race through your mind most of which are unhelpful and others are down-right destructive. Mindfulness practice helps quieten these thoughts and thus allows you to focus on the task at hand in a calm and ordered fashion.

Below I will detail a simple mindfulness exercise which should be done daily. Make this a habit by scheduling 10 minutes during your day when you won't be disturbed.

1. Sit or lie in a comfortable position and notice the feelings and sensations in your body [2mins]
2. Notice that you are breathing. Follow the breath in and out and observe the rise and fall of your chest or abdomen [8 min]
3. If thoughts begin to creep in, notice what they are and gently return your focus back to your breathing.
4. When ready, slowly open your eyes and relax into the rest of your day.

After finishing a meditation session you may feel calm, relaxed or sleepy, these are all perfectly normal. Meditation should be done every day for two months to cause lasting and noticeable change in your life.

There will be days when you simply can't afford to spend more than five minutes meditating and this is fine. If you are extremely short of time you can simply notice your breathing and the sensations in your body while washing-up, queuing or walking to lectures. Performing these short 'presence' exercises will calm down the mind and make you feel more relaxed which will hopefully roll-on to improve confidence, learning and productivity.

Exercise

Alongside mindfulness, exercise is one of the major ways to increase your energy levels and positivity. Flooding your body with endorphins massively increases confidence, happiness and positivity.

I was once told by a British Army physical training instructor that British Army soldiers are contractually obliged to do at least three sessions of physical fitness every week. In his words: 'this could be football, badminton or a triathlon in a tutu – it all counts!', you should follow this advice too!

Free weight training is a popular option amongst males with strength and muscle mass gains boosting attractiveness and confidence. However you

don't need to train like Arnold Schwarzenegger to get the benefit.
On the other side of the coin are cardio exercises such as running or swimming. These are a great way to burn your excess fat and get a solid endorphin rush afterwards which is incredibly relaxing. Running is an easy sport that requires little to no skills to take part in although many people get bored during runs. To overcome this there are many park runs around the country (https://www.parkrun.org.uk) or organised events such as charity 5km runs that you can join with friends to make this somewhat boring activity fun and sociable. You could also download a running app such as Endomondo, post your run times and compete against your friends.

Diet

For most, university is a collection of benders punctuated by the occasional lecture and sporadic assignment. Few people consider the effect of diet on their health, wellbeing and productivity. It is a cliché that you are what you eat, but there is little escaping this fact. Below are some incredibly simple diet tips to keep you at your best during your best years.
Let's start with the obvious: Five portions of fruit and vegetables every day! Yes, you've heard this before. No, it won't ever stop being said. Fruit and veg are essential components to every diet. Correct nutrition will boost physical and mental performance while helping you to maintain an attractive physique. I eat the majority of fruit as a snack between meals. Eating small amounts of food often maintains metabolism and it is especially great if what you are eating has a low calorie content and is nutritious.
Buy your fruit and vegetables in season i.e. don't try and buy apples in June because they will have been shipped in from abroad which costs the shop money which will in turn cost you more money. Furthermore, vegetables that are not in season may be of lower quality and thus less appetising for you. For a guide to the fruit and vegetables that are currently in season see www.bbcgoodfood.com/seasonal-calendar/all.
It is usual to supplement our diet but this can become incredibly expensive and is often unnecessary, so supplement in moderation. There is little need to buy individual diet supplements when a good quality liquid multivitamin such as Floradix should suffice when used alongside cod liver oil liquid or tablets. The cod liver oil is an 'acquired taste' so consider yourself warned!

Positivity and gratefulness

Positive psychology is an area which is being massively emphasised by Cognitive Behavioural Therapists and performance coaches around the world. Positive people are just naturally more likeable and make friends easier with than negative people do. Why would you want to spend your time with someone who continually complains when there are people who have nice things to say and actually make you feel good about yourself.

When you walk along the road your brain takes in a phenomenal amount of information. You will see things such as buildings, grass, trees, stones, litter, cars, people etc. This is just what you see and completely excludes your other four senses! How does your brain know what to focus on? If it focussed on everything you would surely go insane due to the sheer volume of content. The brain has something called the Reticular Activating System (RAS) which is responsible for where your attention lies. If your RAS focuses on something particular then your mind will automatically see this thing everywhere. As an example, when I bought my red Ford Fiesta, I thought I hadn't seen one before. In the following months I must have seen about 500 cars like mine, or so I thought. This little trick of the mind can be leveraged in our favour to create a more positive and happier outlook on life.

Try this exercise: Each evening when you go to bed, write down five things that you're grateful for that happened during the day. Some days this will be easy: 'I went on an awesome date'. Other days this will be much harder, but there will be some positivity there. I'm not saying that genuinely brilliant things need to have happened, just notice the things that made you happy i.e. you enjoyed a cup of tea. Yes, some days that is my highlight!

If you write down the positive things that have happened in your day your mind will automatically focus on them. Over time you will continue to focus on things that you are grateful for and develop a more positive outlook on life. There is another side to this though, if you always look for faults in other people or yourself, then guess what? You would always find them easily!

You have no control over whether or not your mind thinks. Minds think. That's what they do. As well as changing how you see the world using your RAS, you can also change how you interpret things that happen to make thought patterns more productive and less destructive.

Consider this situation, you may have experienced it before. You are walking along the street when you see somebody you know and say 'hi' to them and get totally ignored. What are the two interpretations of this situation?

1. Oh my god, [person x] is so rude. I bet this is because I said that thing to [person y] and they must have told him/her. That's it I'm never trusting [person x] again.
2. Oh, [person x] must not have seen me. Never mind, I'll see them again soon.

Which statement did you align with most? It is natural to assume negative thoughts even though these are likely to be false or if they are counterproductive. Which person would you want to spend time with and be around, the person who said the first statement or the second?

Good news, this kind of positivity can actually be engrained into your mind with gentle practice. Tony Robbins has the Ten Day Positivity Challenge where you try to remain positive about everything for ten consecutive days and if you dwell on something negative for more than 90 seconds, start from day one. This challenge may be particularly difficult if you are used to complaining but with practice it will become easier over time.

Challenge
Remain positive in all situations and don't dwell on negatives for more than 90 seconds. You may wish to enlist the help of friends/housemates to monitor your progress and keep you honest and to offer a forfeit if you fail.

You may have heard that whatever you believe comes true, believe me, this is true! This is called fulfilling the fulfilling a prophecy. You have assumed that something will go badly so your mind does everything it can to make this come true. Let's consider the example of going to a party. You're reluctant to go because you assume that everyone will dislike you or that you won't fit in. This will naturally make you feel nervous most likely will put a scowl on your face. Can you imagine how you will appear to others if you walk into a room scowling? They probably won't like you and assume you're a really unhappy person. Now, let's change this around. How about assuming that you're going to meet some really friendly people who have lots to offer? Do you think you would walk in smiling and relaxed? How do you think this would make others perceive you? It's very likely that they would think you're very friendly and would behave in kind towards you.

Positive thinking doesn't just belong to the realm of socialising. If you assume you will fail, guess what? You probably will. Have you ever heard an interview with Tiger Woods before a game? That man just exudes confidence and positivity. He uses phrases like 'I will play well', 'my game is at its best right now'. Imagine talking to your friends like this, they would think you were incredibly arrogant but this is the winner's mind set.

I want you to consider your mind as an independent being that takes instructions from you so that whatever you decide to put in gets digested and comes out in the form of actions. If you used the phrase 'I'm never going to pass that exam' you're effectively setting yourself up to fail by making your mind focus on failing rather than passing it.

From here on in, I want you to assume you will succeed and phrase everything in the positive. Rather than

"Aw, I'm terrible at differential equations"

you should aim for

"At the moment I don't fully understand differential equations but with work I'll get it".

By this gentle positive act I assure you that within months you will have a better approach to learning and also won't avoid revising previously-loathed subjects.

The weekly plan

If you know what you're going to be doing before you do it then it will be easier to do it. Does that make sense? Coming from an upbringing of total disorganisation and chaos, the idea of creating a plan to get something done seemed time-consuming and unproductive to me. Why would I need a plan to go about my day? I seem to make it through okay, don't I? This wasn't actually true. My organisation was so bad I didn't know when or where my tutorials and labs were which led to me depending on others.
At the moment life may seem calm but have no fear there are forty years of working life ahead of you which will become unbearably stressful at times. When you become overwhelmingly busy having a schedule and a plan of attack will save you from burnout.
Last year learnt about the weekly plan and my life has never been the same since.
Making a weekly plan is done in four stages. I recommend finding a fixed time during the week to achieve this task – Sunday evenings appear ideal as they are both at the end and beginning of the week.

Step one: Review the previous week

It is important to discuss what happened in the previous week. What went well, what didn't and why? If you were to live that week again, how would you do it? Look at your goals from the previous week (see step three). Did you achieve them? If not, why not?
The questions above provide a structure for your 'post-match' analysis. This process may appear time-consuming but it will help clear your mind and allow you to learn from your mistakes.

Step two: Bullet point tasks for the coming week

Essentially this is a 'to do' list for the week. Just write bullet points for ten minutes and make sure you have covered everything. Don't move until the ten minutes are up, there are still thoughts that will come out…just be patient.

Step three: Set weekly goals

Yes, goals are back! Form your to do list into goals to achieve during the following week. If it helps, put these under headings such as fitness, social life, work etc. For example, I have a fitness goal that says 'bench press 80 kg'. You may wish to order these in terms of priority to ensure the most important tasks are completed first.

Step four: Planning

Once you have created your goals, it's time to arrange when you're going to achieve them. Take your calendar and create time-slots for when you will work on each task or goal. A point to note is that if this activity is in a distant location, you will also need to schedule-in travel time.
Once you have time-slots for work and social activities, ensure that you make time for yourself to do nothing. It's important to be productive as this gives you purpose, but it is equally as important to have time to relax otherwise you will most likely experience burn-out which is unpleasant to say the least. If you do find yourself becoming overwhelmed, just go back to the 'De-stress: Relaxation and mindfulness for learning and happiness' section above.

Challenge

Use weekly planning for the next three weeks. Ensure you spend at least an hour covering all of the steps. Notice how productive you feel and write in the following week's journal.

2 EXAM REVISION TECHNIQUES - WORK SMART NOT HARD!

It is natural to feel some nervousness about impending exams but I can promise you this: The world will not stop turning and you will not stop breathing if you don't succeed. What I can promise you is that if you don't work hard (40 hours per week) you will not achieve your best and although you may not fail, you will undersell yourself to prospective employers. Although the majority of graduate employers are not solely focussed on grades why should they take someone with a 2:1 when there is another candidate with a 1st class degree who has the same skill set as you? Consider that there are many more graduates than there are jobs so you need to stand out and having a 1st class degree will get you there!

Your dominant learning style

It has been known for nearly three decades that people understand information in several different ways which are crudely categorised as kinaesthetic, aural, visual and reading/writing. For kinaesthetic learners, their preferred learning style (or the one that would help information go into their brain) would be something to do with touch. With reading, that could mean running their finger along the page with the words or by learning to fix things with a hands-on approach. Aural learners may find that they can understand a problem purely by hearing it discussed in a lecture or discussing it with others. Visual learners will use graphs, images and sketches to understand a problem. Reading/writing learners will find information easier to digest through reading material and headings as well as copying it out onto a page.

It is crucial that you understand which learning type is most appropriate for you. Online tests can be taken to get this result (http://vark-learn.com/the-vark-questionnaire). You will find that people have one dominant learning type and one, or more, secondary/tertiary ones.

By understanding what learning type works best for you, the time spent revising a subject can be drastically reduced or made less tedious. Furthermore, you will also find that by learning with your dominant style, you can make the knowledge stick for longer with little effort.

Flash cards

Flash cards have stood the test of time in learning and education and are an example of a visual learning technique. Short, succinct definitions can be easily revised and games can be made with course mates make the learning more competitive, social and fun!

Flash cards are cheap, mobile and can be used anywhere from the train to the toilet (never admit to this). Other similar visual aids are larger posters (A4) which can be put up around your room so that they are seen many times in a day. I did this for some A-level maths equations and still remember them a decade later.

One excellent tip I did learn to help reduce the amount of time spent of flash cards was the use of daily, weekly and monthly tubs. From the beginning of your course write all of the salient points you learn on to flash cards. Get three small pots to house your cards and write 'daily', 'weekly' and 'monthly' on them. Review these flash cards and for those you get right, put them in the weekly tub, those you don't remember place them in the daily tub. Now, as the name suggests, if you get a flash card right move it to the next pot along and review them either daily, weekly or monthly depending on the pot! Not only will this reduce the amount of cards you need to look at but it will also help you commit things to your long-term memory.

Some learning experts suggest that to help to commit information to long term memory, flash cards should be viewed just before getting into bed.

Make a song and dance about it!

Actually make a song and dance about it. This is a massive plus for aural learners. It is human nature to remember obscure things more than every day events. Do you remember your entire walk to lectures yesterday? Probably not, because it is unlikely that anything interesting happened to you. When something is different, scary, exciting or just provokes emotion, it is remembered well.

If you have something to remember that is wordy, i.e. a definition or speech, try changing the words slightly so they fit into a tune that's easily stuck in your head. An amazing version of this is The Declension Song which can be found on YouTube and was created by Sister Anna Roberta. It is much easier to remember facts if they are made enjoyable or into an easily memorable tune.

Highlighters

We have all seen people whose notes are an indecipherable technicolour arrangement due to an overuse of highlighters. I definitely do not condone this and it may in fact confuse you more than help you. As a visual learner, I have found that writing about particular subjects in a colour-coded manner i.e. red pens for one aspect of a subject and green for another, does actually help my memory.

The real three R's: Repetition, repetition, repetition!

I cannot stress (repeat?) this enough, repetition is the key. Although some learning styles will help your understanding of a subject, if you only go through it once or twice, it may never get internalised. Cover a subject at least seven times to make sure it is internalised.

Quizzes

Competition is a great thing, especially in learning! Gather a few keen course mates together and get into teams. Take it in turns to ask each other course-related questions. If you wish to turn this into a drinking game!

Quizzes are advantageous because they require you to understand an area well enough to ask questions on it. I didn't truly understand some aspects of structural mechanics until I taught the subject, then I absolutely needed to know it! If you aren't motivated enough to organise a full-blown quiz, throw questions at your friends as you walk around the house or on your way to lectures. Again, this is making use of time that would otherwise potentially be wasted.

Learning as a group may be embarrassing for some because they don't want to be seen to be wrong. Dismiss this notion from your head immediately; it's just your ego talking! As soon as you get an answer wrong in front of people, you will remember the answer for years to come.

Start at the beginning

For many, their exam revision begins two weeks before they sit the exam. Obviously this is not ideal as it causes unnecessary stress in the final days which inhibits memory function and the subject enjoyability (yes, this is important!).

The message here is to begin your revision at the beginning of the semester, and here's how. When you attend lectures, tutorials and seminars you will generate notes or question solutions. It is tempting when you get home from a tutorial/lecture/seminar to throw the paper in a draw or folder and continue to go about your day. As much as you think you have understood the material you just covered, this may not be strictly true.

Once you have arrived home from your session, take your notes out and re-write them completely. This performs two major actions: firstly, when you're writing at speed your handwriting can be illegible, and secondly, the information is being seen for a second time in close succession which is essentially a mini revision session. Furthermore, your notes can be restructured allowing you to order them as you see fit. And finally, when covering a topic for a second time, you notice holes in your understanding that you didn't previously see. Do not ignore these! Search online for the answer or e-mail your lecturer and ask for a 10 minute meeting to discuss the gap in your knowledge, they will usually oblige or direct you to somewhere helpful.

Other resources

This book is not intended as a revision, or study, guide but a means of helping you make your life more productive and help you achieve your potential. In Chapter 1: the concept of using audio books during 'dead time' was proposed to expand your knowledge of a variety of subjects. Why not make audio recordings of your revision notes so that you can listen back to them during otherwise wasted time? Or you could download an audio book on accelerated learning techniques, for this I strongly recommend Accelerated Learning Techniques by Brian Tracey. Although somewhat dated, this book contains a plethora of tips and tricks to improve your memory and subjects you like.

3 MAKING THE PRODUCTIVE USE OF YOUR FREE TIME

The student life is reputed for being a time of wild party, and I completely agree that it should be. The majority of those who have been to university have partied until they dropped and are now highly respected subject matter experts in industry and academia and, if you so choose, you should be no different. I have added this section as a general guide to life outside of your studies.

Some may not need the following material as it covers the basics of living, socialising and playing nicely with others but it is added because, as you will see over the next few years, many people don't have these basics and will continue to make social errors and party fouls that will upset others and knock their own confidence.

Living with others: How to play nice

At this point I am assuming you have moved into student accommodation of some sort or another and are sharing with a variety of people you have never met and wouldn't normally associate with.

As you will find in later life while living with friends, partners, husbands and wives; we are all very different. Some find it appropriate to sing in the shower and others consider it to be a mortal sin. Some people wait until the bin is overflowing before emptying it and some will regimentally empty it every three days. I going to use a word and I don't want you to be scared of it, ready? Compromise!

There is no doubt that we all like getting our own way and this is fine but when living in close-quarters with other people who may have very different values to our own, individual priorities must take second place to the collective happiness of the household.

The dos and don'ts of blissful cohabitation

The predictably obvious list below is a collection of ways to build bridges as well as to start wars. Most people wouldn't consider doing half of the don'ts on this list but as you will find out, people can be unintentionally annoying. This list has been added to this book for your use as well as for your amusement.

Do

- Wash up after eating. It is painful for anyone to chisel your two-week old chop suey off a plate that's been festering under your bed.

- Apologise when you've annoyed a housemate. According to the Prophet Elton John, sorry seems to be the hardest word – and it is. For some reason, probably ego, many of us find it difficult to apologise. Simply, "I'm really sorry, [name], that I threw up on you. It won't happen again" can be the difference between keeping and losing a friend. Plus, after a few months (possibly years in this case) you can remind them and laugh about it.

- Consider others at shower time (no, not like that). If most of your house has to be at 9am lectures limit your shower time to less than 10 minutes. Yes, this is very possible.

- I shouldn't need to write this but…take regular showers. It is beyond me why people don't shower at least every 24 hours. Have you ever tried to make conversation with someone who just smelt awful? Love your housemates, shower often!

- Respect other people's time. If you are meeting friends, turn up on time.

Don't

- Steal fridge space. This is a commodity that many would die for, particularly if you have a small fridge-freezer combo. Keep to your shelf – don't be that guy. I once lived with someone who took up the majority of our tiny freezer with ice cream so everyone else had to go shopping more often because their food went off sooner.

- Sing 'Wonderwall' at 3 am when you know your housemates have lectures at 9 am.

- Leave the shower filled with your hair. Going in the shower after someone who has practically shed their winter coat is beyond disgusting. Before you leave the bathroom, quickly run water over the area to ensure that there is no evidence of your shedding. This will save people unnecessarily hating you.

- Interfere with the thermostat unless consulting others. Students have bills that they want to keep as low as possible; this is an age old truth. If you're cold, throw on a jumper or buy a fluffy dressing gown (warning: they are not sexy).

-Assume people get your sense of humour, especially if it is fairly controversial. Some people are sensitive and may take offence at things you consider rather bland, so reserve the offensive or 'edgy' humour for very close friends who actually know that you're joking.

I hope that the list given above was completely obvious and you sighed or said 'well, duh' out loud at least once, this means that you are very socially conscious. If some of the points were entirely new concepts to you, it's time to make a change. You don't need to be particularly nice or special for people to like you or to get along, you just shouldn't annoy them.

Socialising for awkward people

Socialising is not only fun but it can be a great way to create a personal network. Having a network is essential in later life because it will help you easily find jobs from friends rather than going through employment agencies who may take a cut from your pay. Networking will also open up a wider range of options in your social life leading to more fulfilling 'free time'.
When you go into full-time employment, communication will be one of your most valuable assets. During interviews or early stages of work your employer will be considering whether they can leave you alone with a client without you making them feel awkward or being inappropriate. When people feel uncomfortable in conversation, this feeling is felt by the person they are speaking to. If you lack confidence or just wish to hone your socialising skills the following section should provide sufficient help.

Smile

Yes, you may have guessed that people like being around happy and positive people. I have spoken to hundreds of engineers at conferences around the world and very few had what I would call 'people skills'. There were a handful of people whose face and name I remembered because they were so pleasant to be around.
Remember that smiles are contagious. If you approach someone with a scowl they probably will hesitate rather than speak to you. To test this theory I once gave a presentation and asked the audience to look bored, uncomfortable and disinterested. It was the hardest speech I have ever given in my life and from it I learnt how important human feedback is in

conversation. Smiles make you smile, they aid relaxation and create positive emotions in the person smiling as well as the people seeing one. Before you go to talk to someone ensure that you are already smiling or at least look happy.

Be interested in the other person

It is natural to want to discuss yourself and your life because you are the most important person in the world to yourself. However, have you considered that everyone else feels the same? What you think is important may not even register to another person at all. As a test, notice the amount of times you say 'I', 'my' or 'me' in a day.

Have you ever met a person who made you feel genuinely important or special? Perhaps they asked you about an event in your life that you mentioned in passing the last time you saw them and they remembered! Maybe this made you feel truly special and important, so why not pass this feeling on to others by asking them about their life or what they enjoy doing?

It may become the case that you get people mixed up or forget the goings on of others - this is inevitable because we lead such busy lives and may communicate with hundreds of people per week. However, if you know that you're due to see an old friend soon, why not keep an eye out for their Facebook or Instagram posts so you're abreast with what's happening in their life and what's important to them and then talk to them about it?

Don't feel like getting this information is 'creepy'. They've deliberately put this information online so that their friends can share in the experience too!

Don't feel the need to be right

Sometimes you will be talking to someone and they will just be plain wrong about something. What is your go-to response here? Do you have an overwhelming urge to correct them? If you feel this urge, suppress it at all costs!

Correcting someone may make you feel big, clever and superior but this will make the other person feel small, resentful and argumentative. If you simply cannot control yourself don't be abrupt in correcting others, just say something like 'oh, I thought it was [correction], perhaps I am wrong' and move on.

Remember, you don't need to be right all of the time, being wrong occasionally doesn't reflect badly on you as a person and people generally dislike smartarses anyway. Plus, if you admit that you may be wrong, people are much more likely to take on your viewpoint as they will consider it 'non-threatening'.

Remember their name and use it

People love hearing their name used in conversation. When possible use a person's name during conversation to keep them interested and focussed on what you're saying. Obviously there is also the issue of overuse, so restrict name use to less than twice in a sentence.

If you don't catch a particular person's name when you first meet them then just ask them to repeat it. It's less offensive to ask a person to repeat their name in the first few minutes than to ignore it, get it wrong or ask a few hours/weeks/months later!

People are flattered when you remember their name, especially if you only met them once! Like it was said above, if you make people feel special, they will gravitate towards you and respect you more.

There are several techniques to help when remembering names

1. Repetition

This is my favourite method as it requires minimal cognitive effort and minimises the time between hearing and learning. When speaking to someone, I ask their name and repeat it in my head about 20 times in a row. To help hold it in memory I perform the repetition again after a few minutes.

2. Association

Association is simply to associate the appearance, characteristic or name of the person you want to remember to something, or someone else's, appearance or name. If a person looks like someone else I know I link them this way. For example, a member of my hockey team looks like the former Wolverhampton Wanderers FC legend Steve Bull…and his name is Steve. This name was forever memorised. Perhaps you want to remember a girl's name, say it's, Claire. What does she look like? If she has curly hair you could use the association of 'Claire with the curly hair'. Obviously keep these associations to yourself as they may offend, but they will come in useful throughout life.

Challenge

Remember the name of every person you meet this week and use their name during conversation.

Challenge

Make casual small talk to cashiers in shops. Try simple phrases such as 'how are you?' Or 'how's your day going?'
Small conversation starters may lead to longer conversations. If you see these people regularly you will live in a world where you there are friendly faces everywhere you go.

Alcohol and other misadventures

Now children, I'm going to talk to you about a very special subject called 'alcohol'. For those who don't know, alcohol is a chemical that is consumed for social lubrication purposes that promotes forgetfulness, cringe worthy behaviour and awkward mornings-after. It is quite likely that you will drink alcohol at university and if you don't, more power you. Fortunately students generally have limited financial resources so regular excess consumption is fairly difficult to achieve.
Basically the advice is this: At worst drink alcohol less than three nights per week. Try and take days in between and always eat before you go out (no it isn't cheating!). Always avoid being the guy/girl who gets wasted while everyone else is sober – no one likes that person and there's always the risk of committing serious party-fouls while in that state. Make a game out of trying to be the soberest person in your group the whole night – don't worry, it won't last long!

Pro tip

I have learnt from visiting friends around the country and drinking in new cities is that you always need a copy of the address you're sleeping at written on a piece of paper in your back pocket. Phones get lost/stolen/die but good old-fashioned paper will usually last an evening stuffed into the back of your jeans. Even if you're so wasted that you cannot speak, just hand the address to a taxi driver and you'll be on your way!

Sport and societies

Sport has played a significant role in public school education throughout the last few centuries, and for good reason! Playing sport can increase your fitness, physical courage and communication skills which are all highly valuable to anyone looking to be successful in life.

Team socials and social lives

In the world of work, technical skills will only get you so far and it is the leaders of the world who make the most money. Being an active part of a sports team or society will ensure that you increase your confidence in communication but also develop your leadership skills thus making you more valuable to employers.

Statements like 'my drinking club has a [insert sport here] problem' are fairly true in the case of most university sports teams, and this isn't necessarily a bad thing. Sports clubs have regular socials and having another group of people to socialise with will ensure that you are exposed to a wider range of 'world views' which is one of the main aspects of the university experience.

Assuming that you're just too lazy to play sport or are unable to due to an injury or disability, there are still societies available. Most universities have around 100 different societies: Some of the more obscure ones that I've ever heard of was the 'Bondage society' (BondageSoc) at the University of Birmingham, UK. Apparently someone in the Guild of Students had to approve a risk assessment for a BondageSoc field trip into the woods...each to their own.

The beauty of societies is that they are a group of people who love the same thing as you! Be it cheese tasting, tea drinking or bondage, there is usually something for everyone. If you can't find it, create it! Check the rules of your Students' Union, but it is likely that you will need less than 10 people to form a society and what a great thing to add to your CV 'started the University Bondage Society'?! It shows innovation, courage and leadership. Now that's the kind of person I would employ!

Fitness

Aside from leadership and communication development, the physical aspect of sport is good for you - strenuous exercise releases endorphins which makes you feel more relaxed. During a very stressful exam revision period it will be beneficial to put down the books and head out for a 30 minute run. Try this and notice how much more focussed and willing you are to continue in the revision compared to before the run.

Fitter people by nature are more confident because others find them more attractive but also because they feel 'safer' knowing that they have the strength to protect themselves. For those who severely lack confidence I recommend regular weightlifting or sprint circuit sessions. Weightlifting improves strength, builds muscle more also increases testosterone levels which will significantly increase your vitality, vigour and sex drive. Excellent books such as Starting Strength by Mark Rippetoe will guide you through the fundamentals of weight lifting to ensure that you begin safely and avoid injury through poor form. Other texts such as Bigger Leaner Stronger by Michael Matthews will provide a scientifically-backed guide through form, workout routines and diet.

4 FINANCES

Unless you are funded by a generous parent, guardian or sponsoring company, university life can be a period of mild. To live a full and active life in the modern world, money is essential so below are some ways to help you earn and save money without committing to full-time work.

Living on a budget

Budget generation can be easily done by downloading available spreadsheets online or those found in Excel. One simple technique I developed/stole was to withdraw a fixed amount of cash per week, say £50, and spend only that. Just through the process of handing your beloved money over to someone else is enough to make you restrict or prioritise your spending. Occasionally it will be necessary to use a bank card when paying for things. No problem, just take the amount you spent on your card out of your cash and put it somewhere you wouldn't normally go in your room i.e. a small box. You can now consider this money spent for the week. If you leave this money alone and continue to stockpile it, you will soon have a nice surprise when you are absolutely desperate and in financial crisis!

Generating income – the student way!

Sometimes it is not possible to get enough money from the Student Loan Company to live on sufficiently or perhaps you just have expensive taste. Below are a few methods for generating income during your student years that are relatively unobtrusive to your lifestyle. But remember that these are only suggestions and you can be as creative as you like.

Become a tutor

Tuition is a relatively simple way to make some extra money, the hours are flexible and universities often employ students to work in 'maths centres' on campus. Alternatively there are website such as 'www.tutorhunt.co.uk' and 'www.firsttutor.co.uk' which allow you to sign up and offer your services online. Most websites will require identification and references, so get these sorted first to expedite your start date!
You choose your own rates but note that you may first need to start low to build up a regular audience and get the cash rolling.

Invigilation

Some universities employ students to invigilate exams although this is often just for post graduates. If the opportunity arises take it! Invigilation is easy money with no preparation time.

Become a bar tender

Being the student union bartender complete cliché, but from seeing my friend work at one and I think it's a great idea. Think about it. Work on campus, learn a skill that can be used all over the world, you get to meet loads of new people and you can remind your friends about how drunk and embarrassing they were at the weekend. You will also save lots of money because you will avoid getting that drunk because you know that it's an awful look.

EBay selling and passive income generation

I have known a few people that have made some cash through online auction sales although these can be more hassle than they are worth and the return on investment is not guaranteed. However, if you are able to make this work then you may be able to generate a source of income which will require little input from you, leaving more time for revision...or play!
Have a think about your skills, experiences and hobbies and determine whether you can create a mechanism of generating passive income or service. Read The 4-Hour Work Week by Timothy Ferriss for guidance on how to create a passive income 'muse'.

Where to get things that are cheap or free

It is not always possible to make enough money to live as you would like however there is the option of reducing your outgoings by changing where you spend your money.
Although supermarkets are convenient, they charge a premium for items which can be found much cheaper elsewhere. To reducing outgoings, I cannot recommend local markets enough. Most cities or towns will have a market that is open at least twice per week. Although not entirely convenient in terms of timing, you could always add this to your weekly plan to ensure that you make time for a trip to the market.
Markets are usually very vibrant places which bring a massive variety of people from all nationalities together. Personally I walk around markets for fun: where else can you see cow lung or catfish for sale?
I think that every self-respecting student home should have at least one

item of furniture either taken from a skip or obtained from Freecycle.com – the latter is preferable. Freecycle.com is a website where people can offer goods to others' for free instead of dumping them. Note however that some of the more desirable items will be snapped-up quickly.

5 EMPLOYABILITY

It is wise when beginning university, like with all things, to start with the end in mind. Consider questions like what industry do I want to work in? What am I good at? And more importantly: What am I not good at?

Grades are important to some extent but they are not the be all and end all – most employers will tell you that. If you have work experience and a good network of contacts, most employers will snap you up.

Imagine the choices you make with regard to how you spend your free time as being scrutinised by prospective employers in an interview: So Mr X, why did you spend the summer sleeping on your sofa rather than working to get money or experience? It sounds excessive but it will steer you in the right direction.

Tailoring your behaviours to positive actions will breed success over time. This chapter is based around the job advert presented on the next page. Each following section will discuss different means of increasing your employability with reference to the job advert.

A typical job description

Below is a typical advert for an aerodynamics engineer. The role itself is not especially important but it is important how you interpret the advert. Read the advert twice and try and determine the skills and competencies that are being asked for.

Job Title: AERODYNAMICS ENGINEER

There is an opportunity to join the aerodynamics group, initially working on a key missile project, but with further opportunities to work and influence a large number of products, concepts and research. Within this role you would find yourself at the forefront of aerodynamics and be a member of a team delivering innovative solutions in a wide range of scenarios.

Role Description
Working as part of the aerodynamics team you will be involved in the aerodynamic design, characterisation and assessment of airframes. This will involve the use of semi-empirical, computational fluid dynamics and wind tunnel testing methods for aerodynamic simulation as well as a suite of performance analysis tools.

What does this mean for you?
You will be able to work at the cutting edge of aerodynamics as part of a team of specialist engineers. This will include close working with other disciplines within the company such as mechanical design and guidance, navigation and control, as well as external organisations, wind tunnel providers and universities. As such this role is likely to involve some travel within the UK to liaise with these disciplines and organisations.

What's great about us?
You will be joining a team of approximately twenty engineers who form a world class aerodynamic design capability. This team have a broad range of niche and multi-disciplinary skills and are involved in a wide range of activities, providing opportunities for working on and influencing the company's portfolio from the initial research and concept phase, through maturation and development, and into in-service support.

What are we looking for?
Extensive experience of semi-empirical, CFD and wind tunnel test techniques ideally focussed on high-speed aerodynamics. A first/second class honours degree in aerodynamics or a related subject with solid relevant working experience and a desire to get involved in innovative research and proven record of delivering results to time, cost and quality.

What would you get out of it?
Competitive salaries, flexible working, paid overtime (subject to level), a comprehensive pension scheme, sporting activities, fantastic site facilities, bonus schemes, and superb learning and development opportunities.

Placements

Most universities offer degrees that involve a placement year. Placement years are incredibly useful for a few reasons:

- Work experience in your chosen field is gold dust for future job applications. Why take on an applicant who has never even worked in the particular industry? You will save your employers time and patience by already knowing how things work.

- The field of work may not be for you. There is no point spending the next 40 years of your life doing something that makes you unhappy. Better to find out sooner rather than later. Before you worry that you've wasted a few years of your life remember that a lot of skills at the early career level are transferable!

Going back to the aerodynamics engineer role above, the advert clearly states that 'solid relevant working experience' and 'proven record of delivering results to time' are required from the applicant. It is fairly obvious that both of these boxes can be clearly checked during the majority of relevant placement years.

Sometimes it is not always possible to get a placement but if you did work at your Students' Union bar for the last three years, this will show that you're not work-shy and can be consistently relied upon which makes you valuable to an employer.

Module choices

Be wise with your module choices and make choices that reflect your desired field of work (assuming you have one) and don't take them just because your friends are. In your early years of university it is uncommon to have much choice on your modules but as things progress students often have the opportunity to specialise through module or projects. In the 'What are we looking for?' section very specific skills of 'semi-empirical, CFD and wind tunnel test techniques' are desired. If you knew what field you wanted to be in after you graduated you should tailor your final year project or dissertation to this theme. Speak to your tutor if you are unsure.

If you aren't sure what you want to do when you graduate there isn't much to be done: Some people just know and others do not. The best advice is just to choose the modules you enjoy the most while at university and if a related job comes up then at least you have specialised knowledge.

Key skills and personal development

Using the job advert above, or one from your chosen field, note down all of the key skills that are listed – either implicitly or explicitly. For example 'proven record of delivering results to time' can be interpreted as time-management skills. Determine what key skills are most applicable to your industry and take deliberate action to start developing them NOW.

The key thing to note here is that if you begin to develop these skills now while you are still in the early stages of your studies, by the time you graduate you will have these skills honed by the end and will become a highly desirable candidate for most graduate roles.

When in your lectures, look around at your class. Imagine how many of your colleagues actually have the key skills to become an engineer, chemist or whatever. Or do you think they spend every evening watching Netflix and drinking? The fact of the matter is that, by deciding what you want to achieve at the end of your degree very early-on in your studies, you will be able to tailor your behaviours and choices to optimise the final result.

It is common practice in interviews and applications to use competency-based questions. Competency-based questions effectively ask you to give an example of a time when you have used a particular skill. This method of interview ensures that candidates are capable of performing a particular job before they are accepted.

An example of a competency-based question might be 'can you name a time when you worked well in a team?' or 'can you tell me about a time when you came up with a solution to solve a problem?'

Pro tip

Save yourself some time on job applications by having a pre-made selection of generic competency-based questions that you can quickly paste into an application website.

I once knew someone who went for a job in one of the highest paying graduate schemes in the UK and she got asked for example after example after example to prove her competency. Apparently the interviewer called 'next' when she hadn't finished her current example! Without numerous prepared examples she may not have got her dream job.

The idea behind this book was to encourage you to saturate yourself with positive and productive experiences from the very beginning of university. This way you will have three years of leadership/organisation/interpersonal skill development experience which will help you make judgements in life. The quality of the decisions that we make are not necessarily due to your intelligence but in fact are largely down to our previous experiences. Obviously mistakes happen, but the more you make or witness, the better your judgement will become.

People skills

Making friends, socialising and influencing people may be second nature to some, but like watching Bambi walk on ice for others. Being able to easily and effectively communicate with others is essential and there are few jobs that pay well and require little or no human interaction. Chapter 3 covered basic inter-personal skills which will have you well on your way! Remember that these skills are not developed over night, which is more reason to begin using them immediately.
As you wish to climb the corporate structure or even start up your own business, communication with others will play a pivotal role in your ambitions. Communication with others was something I neglected and didn't take seriously in my earlier life and sorely regret it. Take the time now to get this right.

Public speaking

How do you feel about public speaking? Does the idea of standing in front of a room full of your peers make you quake, sweat and want evacuate your bowels? This is perfectly normal for most people as public speaking is the most common fear after dying. To get used to this terrifying ordeal and make it seem commonplace to you, I recommend joining a public speaking group such as Toastmasters International.
Toastmasters meetings are usually held every two weeks and members are given meeting roles, rehearsed or impromptu speaking roles. I became a Toastmaster two years ago and my confidence has skyrocketed. Previously I would stumble and quake in front of a room full of people, whereas now I stand confidently, making jokes and laughing. How times have changed.
Imagine being a 21 year old graduate that gave a near perfect presentation at an interview! Speaking and presentation skills will be developed at Toastmasters through practice and feedback. Attending interviews with professional speaking skills will set you far above the rest.

6 SUMMARY AND WHERE TO GO NEXT

In this book I have attempted present my thoughts on ways to improve your productivity, organisation and wellbeing. The concepts discussed in this book come from personal experience and work well for me but some things may work better for you. I implore you not just to read this book but take action. Remember that even very small changes now can become significant over time – so get to it!

This book has been deliberately kept concise to ensure that you spend your time making changes and not sitting in a room reading! At the end of this book is a list of further reading for each chapter. Again, this reading may not be for everyone but I offer them to you as a resource so you can improve yourself, lead a happier life and contribute more to the world.

ABOUT THE AUTHOR

Clifton Reed is currently a Research Fellow in aerodynamics at a 'Red Brick' university in the UK. He is passionate about encouraging others to achieve their potential.

Printed in Great Britain
by Amazon